YOUR KNOWLEDGE HAS VALUE

Harry Taylor

The figure of the exceptional worker and its reflection of the American perception of normalcy in Davis' "Life in the Iron Mills"

GRIN Publishing

Bibliographic information published by the German National Library:

The German National Library lists this publication in the National Bibliography; detailed bibliographic data are available on the Internet at http://dnb.dnb.de .

Imprint:

Copyright © 2011 GRIN Verlag GmbH
Print and binding: Books on Demand GmbH, Norderstedt Germany
ISBN: 978-3-656-35327-0

This book at GRIN:

http://www.grin.com/en/e-book/207919/the-figure-of-the-exceptional-worker-and-its-reflection-of-the-american

GRIN - Your knowledge has value

Since its foundation in 1998, GRIN has specialized in publishing academic texts by students, college teachers and other academics as e-book and printed book. The website www.grin.com is an ideal platform for presenting term papers, final papers, scientific essays, dissertations and specialist books.

Visit us on the internet:

http://www.grin.com/

http://www.facebook.com/grincom

http://www.twitter.com/grin_com

Harry Taylor

'De profundis clamavi'… analysing the figure of the exceptional worker in Davis' *Life in the Iron Mills,* and its reflection of the American perception of normalcy.

This essay examines the role of the 'exceptional worker' in Davis' realist novella *Life in the Iron Mills,* and what this figure implies regarding contemporary American perceptions of normalcy and class identity. I posit that the capitalist class divide propagates a popular amoral 'normalcy' that consists of a simultaneous fear of the 'human commodity' and a deliberate disacknowledgement of the inhumanity that is the product of the spiritual 'reduction' of the poverty-stricken labour classes. The figure of the 'exceptional worker' in *Life in the Iron Mills* is cynosurial with regard to recognising and supporting this line of reasoning, and is represented most evidently by Hugh Wolfe (an impoverished labourer); as such he will function as the principal object of our examination. How then can we best observe and analyse Hugh? It is clear that viewing him in isolation as an indirectly didactic literary character would be overly reductive, and so we must endeavour to consider Hugh Wolfe as a product of his conditions – conditions rooted in the apathy of class identity and ensured survival by the same skewed perceptions of normalcy that propagate and reinforce their existence. In order to analyse the notion of 'normalcy', we must first recognise and identify it objectively in terms of the contextual intent of the essay. When 'normalcy' is referred to, the term pertains to a set of societal circumstances which are accepted and adopted into the attitudes and expectations of the American people. When discussing 'normalcy', we are considering the way in which the national populace collectively accepts a set of quintessentially capitalist values - which we aim to show are inherently amoral and destructive.

With this in mind we must move to consider the basis of such a notion, beginning with the claim that an amoral 'normalcy' is essentially two-fold, and depends on fear born of class elitism as well as a disregard for the humanity of the labour classes. It is the latter of these two elements that will initially be examined, as it is arguably the most evident when viewing the life of an impoverished labourer through the realist lens of Davis' prose. The way in which the conditions of the labour classes, and most notably Hugh, are disregarded as normalcy by the more elevated strata of society

(3,144 words)

reveals an apathy that transcends attitudes of personal morality or empathy. It is instead rooted in a deeper and more complex passive acceptance of the workings of an unbalanced contemporary capitalist system, and the commodity fetishism inherent within the struggle for both personal and class identity. It is Hugh's role as a living representation of commodity-driven societal disregard for the working classes that presents to the reader the issue of a potentially amoral system which irrevocably reduces the humanity of the common labourer. In his position as the 'exceptional worker', the figure of Hugh recognises and reveals the disparity between being human and what it is to be someone 'reduced' by the process of production – the latter being the inherently amoral 'normalcy' that we aim to identify and examine. To do so, we too must utilise Hugh as a tool: a representative microcosm of the lowest tier of a capitalist system, a 'tool' make exceptional by his ability to express the despairing and diminished souls of the labour classes through sculpture.

At the heart of the claim that contemporary American 'normalcy' is amoral lies the way in which the capitalist system requires a type of 'forgetting' with regard to the commodification of the labourer. The origin of commodities and the spiritual cost that they take on those who produce them is unconsciously unrealised; it is this apathy which is referred to in this essay as a 'disacknowledgement' of the labourer, and is so central in accepting that the consideration of normalcy is fundamentally and morally skewed. The production of commodities is, in a sense, concealed from the common populace by the way in which commodities undergo a veiling under price. Money masks its own production in the sense that it comes to stand in lieu of the commodity which it represents, and as such the nature and soul of the labourer is nullified since they too are commodities to be owned and manipulated by the system. The foundry workers in *Life in the Iron Mills* are in this way shown to be bereft of their humanity – it has been transferred from them to the product of the manufacturing process. Commodification has inevitably and irrevocably stripped from the labourers that which makes them truly human, and they seem entirely powerless to control the ebb of their humanity into the foundries of the mills and the pockets of the capitalists.

Hugh is exceptional because he expresses otherwise, and creates an emulation of life from the very materials which have stripped the souls away from others. This literal

(3,144 words)

sculpting shows that he has recognised a disparity between what it is to be human and what it is to be someone 'reduced' by production. Although this may initially seem somewhat oxymoronic, the life of the worker is, as we have established, put into the product both spiritually and in an entirely literal physical sense. It is an unclean and imperfect process: korl is the result, and the korl woman carved by Hugh is the consequence of a soul's recognition of its annihilation through commodification. In the same way, the processed 'inhumanity' of the labourer is deliberate – it is 'sculpted' by the transition of the spiritual into the mundane. It is possible here to recognise a parallel in these processes; the literal sculpting of the korl woman by the disaffected 'exceptional worker' is reflected by the requirement of social capitalism to sculpt by 'chiselling away' at the humanity of those at the bottom rung of the class ladder. Commodification is by its nature a process that simultaneously creates and annihilates, "a reality of soul-starvation, of living death, that meets you every day under the besotted faces on the street" (Davis, *Life in the Iron Mills, Or, The Korl Woman*, 1972, 8).

The nullification of the humane in the labourer, the 'starvation' of the soul, is the price of industry. Capitalism depends fundamentally on exploitation of the working classes, an aggressive and direct process of capital generation which disregards the value of labour and the labourer: "capital is reckless of the health or length of life of the labourer" (Marx, Capital, Volume I, Chapter 10, 1867). This 'recklessness' is indicative of the apathy of social superiority with regard to the commodification of the human, which abandons the humanity of the proletariat and leaves him "left to feed his soul in grossness and crime, and hard, grinding labour" (Davis, 9) This is unconsciously permitted to happen by those who profit from the system because it is acceptable to ignore the ugly roots at the fundamental workings of capitalism if you are placed far enough up the money tree that grows from it. In the same way that a type of 'forgetting' is induced by the veil of money, the class divide is magnified and made unbreachable by the way in which the upper classes (the buyers of the product and, by association, the humanity of the worker) 'forget' and disacknowledge the labourer.

(3,144 words)

But how, one wonders, is this gross oversight of the savagery of labour and the brutality of poverty so readily disregarded by the socially superior classes? How is it that the class divide is so vast that the consumer of the commodities is, however well intentioned, naturally inclined to completely ignore the tribulations of the labour classes? The answer is to be found in the aestheticising of conditions, in the picturesque and romantic renderings of proletariat existence which mask the harsh reality of life in the iron mills. This denial of realism is perhaps most evident in the language of the aesthete Mitchell, who demonstrates the way in which his intellectualism and anti-realist inclinations are part of a romantic façade constructed between them and the working classes so that they are able to deny the reality of commodity production and disregard the subsequently compromised humanity and 'soul' of the labourer. Such distortions of perception are evident in his reaction upon observing the proletariat labour over the furnaces: "I like this view of the works better than when the glare was fiercest [.] These heavy shadows and the amphitheatre of smothered fires are ghostly, unreal. One could fancy these red smouldering lights to be the half-shut eyes of wild beasts, and the spectral figures their victims in the den" (Davis, 12). The startling irony is that the 'spectral figures' referred to by Mitchell *are* very much the victims, and the 'den' of the beast that they exist in is the Hell of the labour classes which strips them of their intangible human qualities. He is apparently unaware that the consumers of commodities are buying fractions of the human soul, encroaching upon the realm of the divine alluded to by the fantastical imagery. These are the conditions of the exceptional worker, yet Mitchell denies the realism of his temporary surroundings in favour of the aestheticism which permits him (and the entirety of the consumer classes) a degree of moral distancing between themselves and the origin of the commodities that they covet.

The desire of the aesthete to project an overly intellectualised and romantic sheen onto the harsh realism of Hugh's life and surroundings is further demonstrated following the observation and discussion of Hugh's korl sculpture of a woman, when he reflects upon the figure of Hugh: "'*De profundis clamavi.*' Or, to quote in English, 'Hungry and thirsty, his soul faints in him.'" The irony of this commentary is the stark contrast in nature and meaning between his initial Latin observation and what can only be assumed is a mistranslation on the part of Mitchell. The Latin he quotes is part of the first line of Psalm 170, and in English means 'out of the depths I cry'. In the biblical text the line concludes with an appeal to God (*'ad te, Domini'*), but this is conspicuously absent in Mitchell's usage. This is indicative of the godlessness of the proletariat conditions, and gives weight to the suggestion of the iron mills as being an unholy manner of damnation for the workers who have been stripped of their souls through the process of commodification. The fact that Mitchell's comments on Hugh contain a major mistranslation is highly significant, and the further implications are somewhat portentous. The Psalm excerpt is followed by an incorrect claim that 'in English' the meaning is one of a plea for a more base and material satisfaction. Such an unconscious error could be related to the subliminal desertion (by the upper classes) of the recognition of the spiritual in favour of the material – the cry to God from the soulless depths suggested in the Latin is mistaken for a more base desire for the satiation of hunger and thirst. The error of mistaking scripture reminiscent of an appropriately existential yearning for a literal hunger can be placed quite readily beside the point that the spiritual has been exchanged in the fires of the mills for the commoditised produce of labour – it is quite literally a sale of the soul. The aestheticism of the Latin usage also bestows Mitchell's comment with a certain level of inaccessibility for the workers, who of course would not be able to understand it. It demonstrates the superficiality of aesthetic pretension in the face of a realist landscape: not only could the labourers not understand it, but even Mitchell offers a flawed interpretation to his companions in an attempt to appear enlightened. It is, as previously asserted, a façade which obscures the unpalatable implication that the commodities purchased by the higher classes contain an inextricable element of the labourer's human soul.

Now that we have established that an adherence to a true perception of reality is made difficult due to the façade of romanticism, it becomes evident that it is the flawed perceptions of the upper classes which facilitate a shift in the boundaries of normalcy. It is only as a result of this shift in what is considered to be acceptable by the elitist majority that normalcy is displaced and repositioned to accommodate a disregard for the humanity of the labourer. In this way, it can be suggested that (like the mistranslation) the manner in which reality is perceived by the upper classes is altered due to attempts at over-aestheticising the realist world that they are uncomfortable

(3,144 words)

with. This discomfort indicates an unconscious recognition of the amoral nature of this 'new' normalcy, and confesses a fear of recognising and accepting that capitalism facilitates the meta-spiritual damnation of their fellow man, separated though they may be by the class divide. They fear that they will have to deal with the moral conundrum of having to address the fact that they have dismissed the labourers as tools and artifices of the production process, as much so as the commodities that they generate; the fear of threatening the stability of what for them is a profitable system is also at the forefront of their trepidation. When confrontation is elicited over this subject in *Life in the Iron Mills*, Kirby, the co-owner of the mill and the labourers, denies responsibility: "what has the man who pays them to do with their soul's concerns, more than the grocer or butcher who takes it?" (Davis, 15). To Kirby, so distanced from the labourer, it is simply the way that the system works. It is the same class divide which enables the higher tiers of society to consider the subjugation of the proletariat to be not only normal, but acceptable and justifiable in accordance with the shifting template of anti-morality necessitated by being the benefactors of a capitalist system. The veil of aestheticism is therefore placed over the process of industrial production to shield the societal elite from their fears and moral conundrums, enabling them to adopt an apathetic stance with regard to the dehumanisation and commodification of the labourers. Nobody can afford to burden themselves with a sense of morality which would enable them to accept the realism of the labourer.

The dehumanisation of the workers is a phenomenon that we have already examined, and yet we must now move to consider it in light of the subsequent involvement of Hugh as the figure of the 'exceptional' worker. As previously established, the labourers are simultaneously dehumanised by the very process that they engage in and depend upon to support their own lives; they are living without 'living'. They are caught in a form of industrial purgatory, trapped at the bottom of reality and unable to ascend upwards through the gloom towards a life matching the romanticised ones imagined for them by their social superiors. All they can do is offer silent protest: Hugh sculpts his protest, and his resultant korl woman offers her own inanimate appeal. *'De profundis clamavi'*, and indeed they do – they call from the depths of the purgatory created by them, and for them, as a consequence of commodification. It is

(3,144 words)

as if the remnants of the human soul not yet transferred into the inanimate product of labour want to be recognised, to be rescued from poverty and the hell in which it resides and is steadily nullified.

They wish to reclaim the humanity which is being lost through commodification - something which Deborah fantasises about. However, they face a dilemma, since ironically the only way to escape the bottom rung of capitalism is to have enough money to advance your way out of it – which they do not have despite being morally entitled to. This reasoning is fundamentally Marxist: for profit to be generated from a capitalist system, labour must have been underpaid. Since value is created primarily by human labour, the distinction between the 'price' and the 'value' of a commodity is an inherently dishonest one. The industrial process has literally purchased the life-time of the labourer, and the only way to reclaim it seems to be to reclaim it with money. When Deborah tries to do this in the only feasible way (by stealing it, from Mitchell) it seems to Hugh almost divine and unnatural that something with no intrinsic value contains the power to transform their lives "The money,—there it lay on his knee, a little blotted slip of paper, nothing in itself; used to raise him out of the pit, something straight from God's hand." (Davis, 22). Despite recognising the potential effect of the money that is, according to Marx, allocated unfairly to Mitchell, the thievery results in the imprisonment and eventual death of Hugh – they are not allowed to escape the capitalist cycle. This is normalcy; it shows the harsh reality of the contemporary American system which is enabled and furthered by the acceptance of a class divide - there seems to be an unspoken law that to attempt to transcend your lowly sub-human position and advance beyond the status of being a product producing products means a destabilising of the entire system. All they are able to do is 'cry out from the depths' of the hell in which they reside, their souls having been sold not by them, but by the system they find themselves inescapably embroiled in: "there are moments when… his nature starts up with a mad cry of rage against God, man, whoever it is that has forced this vile, slimy life upon him" (Davis, 9).

In this way we can see the apathy of the upper classes: an unwillingness to face the reality of industrial existence, abandoned in favour of an appreciation of the aesthetic veneer which disguises it. This is together with the fear of being forced to recognise

7   (3,144 words)

that they are the people which 'buy' the souls of humans for the price of whichever commodity they produced. Marshall Berman writes that "to be modern is to find ourselves in an environment that promises us adventure, power, joy, growth, transformations of ourselves and the world-and, at the same time, that threatens to destroy everything we have, everything we know, everything we are…" (Berman, Marshall. *All That Is Solid Melts into Air: the Experience of Modernity*, 15). This is the root of the capitalist's fear of realism; it reveals to them the presence of an amorality that they cannot afford, and which threatens the entire capitalist system. The figure of the exceptional worker in Hugh reveals to the capitalists a 'cry from the depths' of the industrial purgatory inhabited by the proletariat, threatening to make them confront their own sense of morality, but the veil of aestheticism descends and masks the cry in mistranslated rhetoric: "*de profundis clamavi*"…

(3,144 words)

Harry Taylor

Bibliography

Davis, Rebecca Harding, and Tillie Olsen. *Life in the Iron Mills, Or, The Korl Woman*. [New York]: Feminist, 1972.

Marx, Karl, and David McLellan. *Capital*. Oxford: Oxford UP, 2008.

Berman, Marshall. *All That Is Solid Melts into Air: the Experience of Modernity*. New York: Simon and Schuster, 1982.

Dow, William. *Narrating Class in American Fiction*. New York: Palgrave Macmillan, 2009.

(3,144 words)